Presented to

Kay & Wayne

on the occasion of

Your life-changing & life-expanding wedding

With love from

Norm & Carol Berg

Celebrating Love

Copyright © 1993 Mary Hathaway

Published by
Lion Publishing plc
Sandy Lane West, Oxford, England
ISBN 0 7459 2397 6
Lion Publishing
1705 Hubbard Avenue, Batavia, Illinois 60510, USA
ISBN 0 7459 2397 6
Albatross Books Pty Ltd
PO Box 320, Sutherland, NSW 2232, Australia
ISBN 0 7324 0756 7

First edition 1993

Library of Congress Cataloging-in-Publication Data
Hathaway, Mary, 1943–
    Celebrating love / Mary Hathaway. – 1st ed.
    ISBN 0-7459-2397-6
    1. Love–Religious aspects–Christianity. 2. Love–
Biblical teaching. 3. Love–Poetry. 4. Sexual attraction–
Biblical teaching. 5. Sex–Religious aspects–Christianity.
I. Title.
    BV4639.H265 1993 93-8002
    241'.4–dc20 CIP

Printed and bound in Malaysia

Acknowledgments

Photographs by Willi Rauch: pages 7, 10/11, 19, 26,
30, 30/31, 31, 32, 42/43, 44; Lion Publishing: pages
11, 15, 18/19, 37, 38/39; /David Alexander: page 36;
Nicholas Rous: page 20; Telegraph Colour Library:
pages 12, 14; /F.P. Fruchet: page 17; /R. Goldman: page
18; /R.H. Smith: pages 24/25; /Peter Beavis: page 29;
ZEFA UK: pages 20/21; /Vaughn: pages 22/23, 34/35;
/J. Tobias pages 26/27; /P. Ashwood: pages 40/41; /
D. Douglass: page 41; /Rick Diaz: page 43; Tony Stone
Worldwide/Dan Bosler: pages 13, 32/33; National
Maritime Museum: page 40; Neil Beer: page 45;
David Kemp: endpapers

CELEBRATING LOVE

Mary Hathaway

A LION BOOK

Oxford · Batavia · Sydney

INTRODUCTION

Love has many facets. It is impossible to isolate one from another. Love between a man and a woman is a gift of God, and when it is seen as part of the wholeness of love, it is even more beautiful.

For me, romantic love is like a doorway—important in itself, but not much use unless it leads somewhere. It is like one color in a sunset. Each shade is lovely on its own and yet blends into the next to make a more glorious whole.

In this book I have chosen pieces of my writing which reflect these colors as they have touched my life over the years. Some have been very bright and others darker. But I feel each of them, in one way or another, has helped to bring me a little closer to an understanding of love. It has also given me much pleasure to share with you my choice of Bible verses and some of my favorite quotations from other people's writing.

For love is about giving rather than getting, about accepting pain as well as joy. It is the giving of ourselves to something that is bigger than we are, the beginning of a journey that can last a lifetime.

Learning to love is still the biggest adventure that this world has to offer.

Mary Hathaway
February 1993

DISCOVERING LOVE

My heart is like a singing bird
Whose nest is in a watered shoot:
My heart is like an apple-tree
Whose boughs are bent with thickset fruit;
My heart is like a rainbow shell
That paddles in a halcyon sea;
My heart is gladder than all these
Because my love is come to me.

CHRISTINA ROSSETTI

There are four things that are too mysterious
for me to understand:
an eagle flying in the sky,
a snake moving on a rock,
a ship finding its way over the sea,
and a man and a woman falling in love.

FROM THE BOOK OF PROVERBS

A quiet look

Love is a quiet thing,
a quiet look, a quiet meeting
of quiet eyes in mutual greeting,
love is no wild thing.

Love is a healing thing,
a healing joy, a deeper giving,
a healing power in the whole of living,
love is no fearful thing.

Love is a restful thing,
a rested mind, an interweaving
of hearts in giving and receiving,
love is no anxious thing.

Stir not up nor awaken love until it pleases.

FROM THE SONG OF SONGS

Love is like spring
warming the ground to birth,
making all things possible.

L OVE IS

The impossible adventure

We often want love
without love's pain,
and then grumble
that love has passed us by.
But would we have wanted love
at the price love asks
or on our own terms?

Love does not bargain,
it does not bend to diplomacy.
It takes all or nothing.
It might blow you anywhere.
You will never be safe,
if you let love in,
never be safe again.

The power of love

Love is strong,
love will conquer,
never, never
despise the power
of your loving.

God will use it
to work miracles
that will change
the world.

Never despair,
never give up,
God does not waste
a single seed
of love that is
sown in obedience.

Those that sow
in tears shall
reap in joy
and the harvest
will last for ever.

FALLING IN LOVE

Am I in love?

What is being in love? What makes it different from other kinds of loving? Some say it only lasts a short while, but perhaps that is because it was the wrong kind of love in the first place. I'm not sure whether I'm in love or not.

But I can try to size up some of the things about our relationship. I want to love him as he really is, not as I might like him to be. I know I feel like a pricked balloon when he's gone, but when I'm with him, life comes back into focus again. He gives me confidence to do things I could never do by myself. Just having him there means such a lot. He helps me to enjoy life more, as well as supporting and comforting me when times are difficult. I have sat with him when he's depressed and felt wretched because there was nothing I could do to help. I've glowed inside when people speak well of him. I hate being apart from him—I'd rather be near him, even when he makes me angry, than be happy away from him. He's in my thoughts continually, and I know I feel incomplete without him.

Does this amount to being in love?

Love is patient, love is kind. It does not envy, it does not boast, it is not proud. It is not rude, it is not self-seeking, it is not easily angered, it keeps no record of wrongs. Love does not delight in evil but rejoices with the truth. It always protects, always trusts, always hopes, always perseveres. Love never fails.

FROM THE FIRST LETTER TO THE CORINTHIANS

*J*UST THE TWO OF US

I am my beloved's and his desire is towards me.

FROM THE SONG OF SONGS

Summer grasses

From where I lay
the summer grasses made
a hundred patterns,
etched in flowing filigree
against the sky.

Then, it seemed,
they held me
in a dome of light
and bowed their heads
to feel such
weight of love.

For there you were,
beside me—
and the world drew back,
leaving us to walk
alone within
our private kingdom.

Alone together

Alone—together,
together—alone.

Not completely alone,
not completely together,
not having to be silent,
not having to talk,
not having to explain,
not having to ask questions.

Two spirits touching,
yet traveling
in different countries
at the same time,
sharing what they find
but not expecting
to tread in each
other's footsteps.

I used to be troubled
that you could not
follow me,
and when I tried
to enter your kingdom
I could never find the door.
I felt I had failed
in some way because
there was this part of you
I would never understand.

I did not realize then
the need to respect
each other's private world,
the complete acceptance
of the shut door
behind which each
walks alone
with his God.

But now I thank you
for giving me
this precious gift,
alone—together,
the true freedom
of love.

Let there be spaces in your togetherness.
And let the winds of the heavens dance between you.

Fill each other's cup but drink not from one cup.
Give one another of your bread but eat not from the
same loaf.
Sing and dance together and be joyous, but let each
one of you be alone,
Even as the strings of a lute are alone though they
quiver with the same music.

And stand together yet not too near together:
For the pillars of the temple stand apart,
And the oak tree and the cypress grow not in each
other's shadow.

KAHLIL GIBRAN

Don't do anything from selfish ambition or from a
cheap desire to boast, but be humble towards one
another, always considering others better than
yourselves. And look out for one another's interests,
not just for your own.

FROM THE LETTER TO THE PHILIPPIANS

Laughter with love

Laughter with love
rings out with pleasure,

sparkling with fun
like joy set to music.

Laughter with love
is like raindrops on water,

spreading delight
in circles of gladness.

Laughter with love
glows like a candle,

a teardrop of light,
shining with beauty.

Laughter with love
gives me moments of wonder,

your eyes lit with loving,
returning my brightness.

Be happy with those who are happy.

FROM THE LETTER TO THE ROMANS

Grief can take care of
itself, but to get the full
value of a joy you must
have someone to
divide it with.

ANON

I' M   S O R R Y

We know that if we really want to love, we must
learn how to forgive.

MOTHER TERESA

Loving takes so much

Does loving include hating?
I wonder.
Can you love someone deeply
without sometimes turning
against them?
Because loving takes so much—
it takes all of us so that
sometimes there is nothing left.

The true opposite of love is not
hate but indifference.

ANON

Bear with each other and forgive whatever grievances
you may have against one another.
Forgive as the Lord forgave you.

FROM THE LETTER TO THE COLOSSIANS

Not joy only

Love is not love until it hurts
for it is only in forgiveness
that it proves itself.
But how can pain, pride,
anger and tears possibly
be part of loving?

Sometimes the battle seems
too much for us and the vision
of love we once held so dear
seems unobtainable.
Perhaps the foundation stone
beneath all the conflicting emotions
is the genuine desire to love,
not to be wholly content
with things as they are.

For this is not the whole story.
Somewhere, somehow, one day,
we shall find the pain and joy
fitting together at last
into a pattern. And we shall say,
"Yes, we were not mistaken,
this is love—and it is glorious!"

Then we shall be able to see the pain
as part of the whole process
and not give up on our loving
because we think it is joy only.

The love gift

I love listening
to this music
you have given me.
For it is
restful and unusual,
the intertwining
of words
with gently flowing
melodies;
a picture unfolding
in deep, dusky colors.

No other music
quiets my mind
and brings peace
to my spirit
as this your
gift to me.

It is precious
to me because
it is beautiful,
but, most of all,
because you gave
it to me with love.

Shared memory

We walked silently, I remember,
in the stillness
of a summer evening.

Then at the end of the pool
two geese swam by
and in between a host
of little goslings—
it was difficult to count them
but in the end
we made it thirty-five!

"They must be running a
nursery,"
you said and I laughed
because they were so beautiful.

And now in the brightness
of that shared memory
I give thanks for the beauty
of love at ease
and the joy of silent
companionship.

Be always humble, gentle and patient. Show your love by being tolerant with one another.

FROM THE LETTER TO THE EPHESIANS

The hidden places

Who am I to think
that I should possess you?
You do not possess me.
You have my time, my energies,
my love, you have
a very large part of me
but you do not possess me entirely.

For I have my own thoughts
that wing their way
into uncharted places.
Part of me will always be
a mystery to you and
everyone except God.
I give you myself,
but the places in my spirit
where my being is renewed
with love and strength,
these are secret.

And there are hidden places
in all of us.
Part of you should always
be a mystery to me—
only arrogance asserts it knows
another person entirely.

How foolish to even think
that we can possess anyone,
for then we lose all respect
for one another!

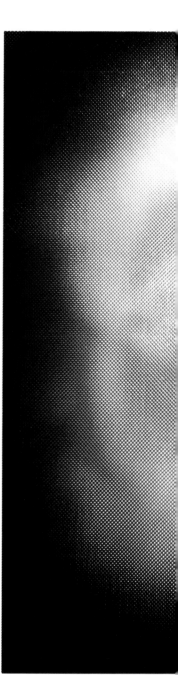

Freedom

To know yourself
is to fly.
Knowing who you are
gives you wings.
Not knowing who you are
puts you in a cage.

To try to be
what you are not
is imprisonment.
No one can
be everything,
so few people
really know
who they are.

N O   B E D   O F   R O S E S

When love grows tired and old

What happens, Lord,
when love grows tired and old?
And vision, once like fire,
grows cold,
and the mind is numb
with lack of sleep
and filled with duties
it must keep
till there is no room
for what it once called its soul—

what happens, Lord,
when love grows tired and old?

A living love hurts. Jesus, to prove his love for us,
died on the cross. The mother, to give birth to her
child, has to suffer; if you really love one another
properly, there must be sacrifice.

MOTHER TERESA

Help to carry one another's burdens, and in this way you will obey the law of Christ.

FROM THE LETTER TO THE GALATIANS

Love for all seasons

Love is
for all seasons,
not just
the vibrant spring
or summer laughter,
with its welcome shade,
but for bringing
to a fruitful place

the purposes of living
and to warm the winter
of our sorrows.

For in every season
of my life
I find new joy in you.

So I love you

As day rejoices in sunrise
as the weary rejoice in rest,
as the lost rejoice in being found,
so I rejoice in you.

As branches belong to the tree,
as light belongs to morning,
as birdsong belongs to springtime,
so I belong to you.

As warmth from the fire welcomes the cold,
as light from the window welcomes the wanderer,
as a child welcomes a birthday,
so I welcome you.

The great essentials of happiness are something to do, someone to love and something to hope for.

ANON

Our love should not just be words and talk; it must be true love, which shows itself in action.

FROM THE FIRST LETTER OF JOHN

U NITED IN LOVE

Love ... binds all things together in perfect unity.

FROM THE LETTER TO THE COLOSSIANS

The mind and the heart

My mind goes free and rises untrammeled
among the stars, but my heart has made its
home in you, for I have chosen to dwell
there. I do not ask you to keep my mind,
only my heart and I believe I have chosen a
safe resting place. For my mind is always
traveling—but how badly my heart needed a
home!

Lamp in the dark

And so we walked
with only the night for company,
and your love glowed
like a lamp in the dark
so that I was warm and unafraid.

And I was filled with gratitude,
for within this sphere of light
I have traveled to many places,
and have seen them lit
by the safety of your love.
You have widened my world
and set my spirit free
to fly up into beauty.

And when it sings for joy
high up above us both,
I pray with all my heart
that it may bring you gladness,
for unless it had its home in you
it could give no music
to the world.

The walled garden

At the heart of a relationship
is a walled garden,
a secret place of hidden beauty
from which both partners
go out refreshed
and which is kept for them alone.

If it is neglected
there is only a wilderness
for them to offer each other,
for a garden untended
goes wild.

But time given
to keeping it beautiful
is time well spent
and will give
increased fulfillment
in every area of life.

If you have built castles in the air, your work need not be
lost: that is where they should be.
Now put the foundations under them.

ANON

All that you are to me

I look across the worlds
that have passed by
since I met you, and see
the point where we began
as dimly as a distant star.

But, at other times,
it seems so near
I could reach out
and hold it in my hand.

I do not always
feel that I love you
as much as I do now,
I know I do not
always remember
how much I owe to you.

But this night I thank you
for all that you are to me,
and am glad that as I face
the future, it is you
who stand by my side.

Love must grow

Love has an infinite heart
and cannot stay in a narrow mind.
It is always sweeping on and on,
always living, growing and becoming.
And those who have stopped
changing and growing
have stopped loving.

We can think we still love
because we continue
to go through the motions.
But where there should be
a garden of joy,
there is only a dusty tombstone
on which is written,

"Love once passed this way
but this heart was too small
to contain it.
It would not dare to grow
and yield utterly to love,
so love had to leave it—
long, long ago."

Broken relationship

I had waited
so long for love,
and then the door opened.
I went through it eagerly—
and found nothing.

The words were there
but not the meaning,
there were all
the trimmings of love,
but no love.

Now, as I look back,
the relationship seems
like an empty shell
or a half-built house
where no life was ever lived.

It seems almost laughable
that I could have thought
it was love—
but I was taken in
because I knew nothing better.

I pray that your love will keep on growing more and more,
together with true knowledge and perfect judgment, so that you
will be able to choose what is best.

FROM THE LETTER TO THE PHILIPPIANS

True love

Let me not to the marriage of true minds
Admit impediments. Love is not love
Which alters when it alteration finds,
Or bends with the remover to remove:—

O no! it is an ever-fixéd mark
That looks on tempests, and is never shaken;
It is the star to every wandering bark,
Whose worth's unknown, although his height be taken.

Love's not Time's fool,
though rosy lips and cheeks
Within his bending sickle's
compass come;
Love alters not with his brief
hours and weeks,
But bears it out ev'n to the
edge of doom:—

If this be error, and upon me proved,
I never writ, nor no man ever loved.

WILLIAM SHAKESPEARE

How do I love thee? Let me count the ways.
I love thee to the depth and breadth and height
My soul can reach, when feeling out of sight
For the end of Being and ideal Grace.
I love thee to the level of everyday's
Most quiet need, by sun and candlelight.
I love thee freely, as men strive for Right;
I love thee purely, as they turn from Praise.
I love thee with the passion put to use
In my old griefs, and with my childhood's faith.
I love thee with a love I seemed to lose
With my lost saints,—I love thee with the breath,
Smiles, tears, of all my life!—and, if God choose,
I shall but love thee better after death.

ELIZABETH BARRETT BROWNING

G IVING LOVE

Loving others

If I do not learn
to love others,
all the rest of my life
is like withered leaves
blown by the wind.

If I do not make
time for others,
all that makes me busy
becomes a useless rushing
and a meaningless waste.

If I do not give
myself to others,
my life shrivels
and I lose all the joy
God has in store for me.

To show great love for God and our
neighbor we need not do great things.
It is how much love we put into the doing
that makes our offering something
beautiful for God.

MOTHER TERESA

Let love make you serve one another. For the whole Law is summed up in one commandment: "Love your neighbor as you love yourself".

THE LETTER TO THE GALATIANS

You can make your living out of what you get, but you make your life out of what you give.

ANON

You can give without loving, but you cannot love without giving.

AMY CARMICHAEL

God is Love

All love like shining paths
leads back to him,

all love like streams of life
flows out from him,

all heights of human love
fall short of him,

all joys of earthly love
are there in him,

like one ray from sunrise
they are found in him,

all love, overflowing,
floods out from him—

perfect love is living
in love with him.

I am convinced that neither death nor life, neither angels nor
demons, neither the present nor the future, nor any powers,
neither height nor depth, nor anything else in all creation, will
be able to separate us from the love of God that is in Christ
Jesus our Lord.

FROM THE LETTER TO THE ROMANS